Shake a Palm Branch

The Story and Meaning of Sukkot

Shake a Palm Branch

by Miriam Chaikin

illustrated by Marvin Friedman

Clarion Books

TICKNOR & FIELDS: A HOUGHTON MIFFLIN COMPANY

NEW YORK

For Jim Giblin and Ann Troy
with deep appreciation

Acknowledgment
With thanks to Rabbi Lynne Landsberg
for reading the book in manuscript form.

Clarion Books
Ticknor & Fields, a Houghton Mifflin Company
Text copyright © 1984 by Miriam Chaikin
Illustrations copyright © 1984 by Marvin Friedman

Printed in the U.S.A.

Library of Congress Cataloging in Publication Data
Chaikin, Miriam.
Shake a palm branch.
Includes index.
Summary: Traces the history and significance of
the Jewish fall festival which commemorates the
wandering of the Israelites in the wilderness and the
festival with which they celebrated their arrival in
the Promised Land.
1. Sukkot — Juvenile literature.   [1. Sukkot.
2. Fasts and feasts — Judaism.   3. Jews — History]
I. Friedman, Marvin, ill.   II. Title.
BM695.S8C53   1984   296.4'33   84-5022
ISBN 0-89919-254-8

P 10 9 8 7 6 5 4 3 2 1

Contents

A race that persists in celebrating their vintage, although they have no fruits to gather, will regain their vineyards.

— Benjamin Disraeli

The Most Joyous Festival

Sukkot is the fall harvest festival of the Jews. Unlike Jewish holidays such as Hanukkah, Passover, or Purim, Sukkot does not celebrate any one event. Rather, it celebrates two phases of Jewish history. Sukkot "remembers," as holidays do, the two important periods of time in the lives of the ancient Israelites — the wandering in the wilderness on their way to Canaan, the Promised Land, and the fall festival they celebrated when they arrived there. The customs of the holiday are a re-creation of those times, a re-enactment. Continuing the tradition links past and present and allows Jews to experience the lives of their ancestors.

The holiday takes place in the seventh month of the Jewish agricultural year, the month of Tishri, sometime in September or October. This is the longest of all Jewish festivals and the most joyous. People *must* enjoy themselves. It is the

ABRAHAM·SARAH

law. The Hebrew Bible, which contains, among other things, the laws of the Jews, says, "You shall rejoice before God for seven days."

Sukkot is the plural of the word *sukkah*. A sukkah is a temporary shelter. This may be a booth, shack, or hut. It may even be a parasol, which gives shade. It may be a tent. *Tabernacle* is another word for tent, and Sukkot is also known as Feast of the Tabernacles.

The first mention of a Jewish festival in the seventh month appears in a book of ancient Jewish writing — the Book of Jubilees. According to it, the holiday began in the time of Abraham and Sarah, some 4,000 years ago. They were the first Jews because they were the first persons to recognize God. They and their clan worshiped God. All other people were pagans, who worshiped idols.

The Book of Jubilees says that Abraham and Sarah and their clan celebrated a seven-day festival in the seventh month at the Well of Oaths, which is located in the city of Beersheba today. Burnt animal offerings, or offerings by fire, were an ancient form of prayer. The celebrants burnt an animal on their altar. They are described as marching around the altar seven times with wreaths on their heads and branches in their hands, giving "thanks to God for all things in joy."

This account is not accepted by Jewish scholars because the Book of Jubilees is not considered to be a sacred book. Only the Bible is sacred to the Jews. And Jewish scholars base their beliefs about the origin of Sukkot on the biblical account, which says the holiday began in Moses' time.

The Wandering

The wandering took place around 1200 B.C.E.
(Jews refer to the period of time which Christians
call B.C. as B.C.E., Before the Common Era.) Led
by Moses, the Jews fled from Egypt, where they
had been slaves. Their destination was Canaan,
the Promised Land. Why did they call it that?
Because God had promised to give them the land
of Canaan. The Israelites stopped at an oasis called
Sukkot. They rested in the shade of its trees and
provided themselves with water. Then, driving
their flocks before them, they set out on their
long journey.

In the seventh month, they encamped. The fall
season had arrived. It was time to celebrate the
seven-day fall festival. The hot, dry days of summer were over. The first light rains were beginning to fall, and that was something to celebrate.
Rain was seen as a blessing. Without the water it
provided, people would die of thirst. Crops could

not grow. Cattle, sheep and goats would have no grass to eat.

Aaron, Moses' brother, was the high priest. He led all ceremonies. To help Aaron celebrate the fall festival, priests put willow branches around the altar. Others held willow branches, which they waved.

The Israelites were not alone in their use of willow branches. In ancient times, people thought the willow tree possessed magic. It seemed to cure people and make them strong and fertile. At times it probably did. Aspirin, one of the greatest drugs ever invented, has ingredients from the willow.

Why the ancient Israelites waved the branches is not known. The waving may have been an expression of thanks. Perhaps the ancients borrowed the movement from the trees. Trees toss and shake in the wind. They seem to be dancing or rejoicing.

In the Bible, trees are often spoken of as a symbol of goodness or joy. Examples from the Book of Psalms are:

Praise ye the Lord, ye mountains and hills,
fruitful trees and cedars. (148:9)

The righteous shall spring up like the palm tree;
like a cedar in Lebanon shall they grow high. (92:13)

Let the heavens rejoice, let the earth be glad,
let the seas roar and the fields exult, then
shall the trees of the forest sing for joy. (96:12)

Aaron also conducted a water-pouring ceremony each day of the festival. He poured water on the altar, in a symbolic prayer for rain. God, the all-powerful, gave or withheld rain.

Before Moses died, he commanded the Jews to obey God's law in the Promised Land and to celebrate the festivals. The Israelites promised to obey.

Celebrating in Canaan

The second event that the holiday celebrates grows directly out of the first and is the next episode in Jewish history. In Canaan, the Israelites became farmers. They and their Canaanite neighbors both worked the soil. But great religious differences separated the two peoples. The Canaanites were idol worshipers. They worshiped Baal, a male god, and Asherah, a female god, as well as other gods. Altars to Baal could be seen everywhere. Beside the altar, stuck in the ground and under a leafy tree, was a wooden pole with a carved face at the top. This was the goddess Asherah.

The Israelites sacrificed animals on their altars. The Canaanites sacrificed animals too, but they also sacrificed their own children. In the law of the Jews, child sacrifice was forbidden. But it was widely practiced among the pagans. Archaeologists have found evidence of the practice.

The Harvest

In the meantime, the Jewish farmers discovered the treasures of the earth in the Promised Land — wheat, barley, figs, dates, pomegranates, olives, and grapes. The grapes could be eaten fresh or dried into raisins, and could be made into wine. The juice of the pomegranate was a refreshing drink. Dates spread on a piece of bread made a delicious meal. Pressed olives gave oil for cooking and for burning to make light. The Jews found much to be grateful for. They worked the earth and marveled over the miracles of food that it produced.

Each year, in the seventh month, the first rains of winter began to fall. The scorched earth of the summer was moist again. Now the farmers could plant their winter crops — wheat and barley. They also had to hurry to gather the crops that were ripening. If the grapes that had been planted earlier were not picked in time, they would rot. Some crops grew far from the farmer's house. So as not to lose time going between the house and the distant field, the farmer built a booth — a sukkah — and lived there till the crops were harvested. At night he slept in the sukkah, and in the daytime he took shelter there from the heat of the sun. In addition to protection, the sukkah provided another advantage. The physical presence of the farmer in the field scared away crop thieves – human and animal.

When the planting and gathering was over, it was time to celebrate, time to give thanks for a good harvest. It was also time to pray to God for rain to nourish the seeds that now slept in the earth.

Some Jews went to local shrines near their homes to celebrate. Most preferred to go to the main shrine at Shiloh, in the north of Canaan. The Tabernacle from their days of wandering in the desert was now located there. The Tabernacle was the holiest shrine because the Ark of the Covenant was housed in it. The Covenant was the law of the Jews, the two tablets with writing on them that Moses had received from God on Mount Sinai. The altar of sacrifice was also located at Shiloh.

Each morning people gathered in the courtyard of the Tabernacle at Shiloh for the morning sacrifice. The high priest, standing at the altar, offered up an ox and a ram to God, to give thanks for the harvest. As Aaron, the first high priest, had done, the high priest at Shiloh poured water on the altar to pray for rain. Helper priests also followed the customs of an earlier time. They placed willow branches around the altar. They marched with branches and shook them.

The night was reserved for entertainment. So each evening, as it began to grow dark, everyone

hurried to the vineyards to watch the dancing maidens perform the harvest dance.

The early names of the holiday were *Hag*, Feast, and *Hag ha-Asif*, Festival of the Ingathering. Because one was duty-bound to have a good time, it was also called *Zeman Simhatenu*, Time of Our Joy.

The Holiday Develops

Over the centuries, new customs were added to the harvest festival of the Jews. David, the slayer of Goliath, was born in Bethlehem. He later lived in Hebron. But when he became king, he made Jerusalem his capital. In doing so, he made Jerusalem the most important city in the land. To increase its importance, he brought the Ark of the Covenant to Jerusalem. Jerusalem was now not only the capital but the religious center as well. The fall harvest festival was the main festival of the year. The pilgrims now came to Jerusalem to celebrate. David dreamed of building a Temple for the ark, to replace the desert Tabernacle. He set the wheels in motion by buying a site for the Temple on Mount Moriah in Jerusalem.

On this site, King Solomon, David's son, built the Temple of which David had dreamed. Solomon chose the fall festival as the time to dedicate the Temple to God. That assured him of the largest possible audience. Jerusalem was never more crowded than during the fall festival.

That year, 955 B.C.E., thousands of pilgrims and visitors flocked to Jerusalem for the double celebration. Not only could they look forward to the merriment of the fall festival, but they also would see with their own eyes the marble and gold Temple that Solomon had built to God. It was said to be the most beautiful building in the world.

Sheep and oxen without number were sacrificed during the holiday. The altar in the Temple court-yard was in constant use. Animals were roasting all day, for seven days.

The rituals were the same as in former years. But the grand Temple called for grander ceremonies. Until that time all priests were descended from the priestly family of Aaron. But now a new class of priest arose — musician priests. They didn't have to be members of any particular family. They needed only to be devout and to possess a talent for singing or playing one of the musical instru-ments of the day — cymbals, lutes, flutes, fifes, and harps.

With a new Temple and new ceremonies, the merrymaking at the fall festival increased year by year. In time, the frivolity became a problem. It seemed that people went to Jerusalem more to eat, drink, and be merry than to thank God for a good harvest. Nor was that the worst of it.

Solomon's Temple

Contrary to the teachings of their greatest leaders, the Jews began to worship idols again. They did not renounce God. They merely added idols to their system of worship.

It was Solomon's fault. He had many wives. Each wife represented another peace treaty: By marrying the daughter of a pagan king, he made sure his wife's father would not make war against him. Since most of Solomon's wives were pagan princesses, they worshiped idols. They arrived at the palace in Jerusalem not only with a dowry but also with the idols they worshiped and a group of priests for the worship service. Solomon did nothing to stop them. Many Jews took it as a sign of approval and began to worship idols again. Asherah posts went up in front of Jewish homes and at Jewish shrines throughout the land.

The idea of worshiping one God had been a long time in taking hold among the Jewish people. Abraham taught the worship of one God to his clan. Moses strove to implant the idea in the minds of the people. But time and again people fell back into idol worship. An idol was a statue that could be seen and touched. The people could not see or touch God. Perhaps they felt they had a better chance of having their prayers answered by a physical object than by an invisible God.

In 640 B.C.E. idol worship was halted for a time. Jews returned to the practice of sacrificing only to God at the fall festival. In that year, King Josiah had ordered repairs made on the Temple. In the course of the work, the high priest found an ancient book in one of the corners of the Temple. It was no ordinary book but a treasure. The book was written by Moses himself. It was the book of Deuteronomy, one of the books of the Bible. It contained the laws of the Jews.

When Josiah read the book, he saw how far the people had strayed from the laws they had promised to obey. He let it be known throughout the land that the book had been found. Then he called the priests and elders together in the Temple

courtyard and read them the laws. The people were ashamed. They had promised to worship only God, and instead they were worshiping idols. They had sworn not to bow down to graven images, and they were bowing down to Asherah posts. The people vowed to Josiah and to each other that they would return to the worship of God.

To help the people keep their word, Josiah banned idol worship from the land and had all pagan idols, altars, and shrines destroyed.

The merrymaking at the fall festival now became less rowdy. The mood of the holiday reached a higher plane. Once again, people thanked God for the fall harvest. The fall festival began to be called also *Hag ha-Elohim*, Festival of the Lord.

Festival Laws Are Assembled

In its long history, Canaan, the Promised Land, was conquered by one foreign power after another. When the Babylonians conquered Canaan in 598 B.C.E., they took most of the Jews captive and sent them to Babylonia. Only some peasants were left behind. They did their best to keep the festivals. But in time they forgot how to celebrate. They remembered only that the fall festival took place in the seventh month.

Around 444 B.C.E., Ezra, a Jewish scholar, arrived from Babylon. He had heard about the sorry state of Jewish life in Jerusalem. And he had come to teach the people the laws and customs they had forgotten. He collected the laws and assembled them so that people would be able to get the information they were looking for.

He also read the laws aloud. On the first day of Tishri, two weeks before the start of the festival, he called the people together in the Temple court-yard. (The book of the Bible called Nehemiah, in chapter 8, tells of this event.) And he read to them from the laws that he had assembled:

And God spoke to Moses saying, Tell the Israelites to celebrate the fifteenth day of the seventh month for seven days. The eighth day shall be a holy convocation.

He read to them how to celebrate and with whom:

On the fifteenth day, when you have gathered in the fruits of the land, take the fruit of goodly trees, branches of palms, boughs of thick trees, and willows of the brook, and rejoice before your God for seven days.

Dwell in booths, so that your children may know that their ancestors lived in booths when God brought them out of Egypt where they had been slaves.

Rejoice in your feast, with your family, your servants, and the stranger, the orphan, and the widow who are in your midst.

When the people realized how much they had forgotten, they began to weep. Then they gathered branches and vines and went to make booths.

The Sages Spell Out the Rules

The people now knew what to do, but not quite how to do it. They needed more information. So Ezra appointed a group of sages to interpret the laws and make rules for the holiday. The sages studied the written laws. They also asked old people about what they remembered of the customs that used to take place: How did your parents celebrate the fall festival when you were small? Did they stand or sit? Did they hold something?

The sages completed their studies. They began to call the holiday *Hag ha-Sukkot*, Festival of Booths (or Tabernacles).

These additional rules were to be followed:

Willows were to be placed upright around all four sides of the altar.

Willows were to be taken in hand and beaten against the floor.

The high priest was to conduct a water-pouring ceremony.

All priests were to march in the procession around the altar seven times, making seven *hakafot* — circuits — around the altar.

People were to hold the *arba minim* — the four species — and rejoice before God with them.

Some points were controversial and had to be debated. One of the four species needed clarification.

The Four Species — Arba Minim

The people were perfectly willing to hold the four species, but just what were they? And how were they to be held? The section of the Bible that Ezra had read to them spoke of a goodly fruit and certain branches. But these were not named.

The sages identified the four species:

The fruit of a goodly tree was the *etrog*. This is a citrus fruit that looks like a large lemon. What made it goodly? It was hardy enough to last seven days, it had a pleasing aroma, and it could be made into marmalade when it was no longer needed.

The palm — *lulav* in Hebrew — was the date palm.

Holding the four species

The tree is native to the land, and dates were a favorite and nourishing food.

The thick tree was the myrtle, *hadas* in Hebrew.

The willows — *aravot* in Hebrew — were known by all and needed no clarification.

The Dispute Is Resolved

Two rules were disputed among the sages, the beating of willows and the water-pouring ceremony. One group of sages said these rituals should not be included because there was no specific law for them in the Bible. The second group insisted the rituals be included. They said these were things that had been done in the past and should continue to be done as a matter of tradition. The ayes won. The victory made later generations very happy. For the water-pouring ceremony grew into a great and extravagant pageant and became the highlight of the festival. It was said at the time that whoever has not seen the festival could not know the meaning of the word *joy*.

Festival of the Water Drawing

In the first century B.C.E. Rome was the great world conqueror. Canaan, then called Judea, was part of the Roman Empire. But the Jews ruled themselves and kept their festivals. And each year in Tishri, the seventh month, Jerusalem was alive with preparations for the holiday. Sukkot could be seen everywhere, on rooftops, beside homes, in open fields.

Pilgrims arrived in the city from all directions. Most came on the road from Babylon, some 600 miles to the east. The road was popular for several reasons. It was built by the Romans and was the best road between the two cities. Roman guards patrolled it, making it safe from bandits. Last but not least, the road was toll-free.

The rich pilgrims arrived with oxen, sheep, and goats to offer up to God. Poor pilgrims brought two pigeons, a sack of flour, or a jar of wine.

Those who arrived on donkeys dismounted at the city gates, for a pilgrim was expected to arrive at a festival on foot. The word for foot in Hebrew is *regel*. The term for pilgrim festival is *Hag Aliyat ha-Regel*, which means "Going Up (to the Temple) by Foot" Festival, or Walking Festival.

The festival program was the same each day: morning sacrifice, prayers, additional sacrifices, study, eating and drinking, more prayers, evening sacrifices – followed by rejoicing.

At sunrise, everyone hurried up the steps of the Temple for the morning sacrifice. The men's section was called the Court of the Israelites. The women's section, up a flight of stone steps, was called the Women's Court. Below, in the courtyard, the high priest and his helper priests stood around the altar.

The activity around the altar was endless as seventy oxen and seventy rams were sacrificed during the holiday period. Why seventy? Because ancient Israelites believed the population of the world to consist of seventy nations. Each pair of animals sacrificed represented a prayer for the welfare of each nation.

After the morning sacrifices came the moment everyone had been waiting for.

Not far from the Temple was the spring of Shiloah. The high priest, leaving the altar with a golden pitcher, went down the steps of the Temple and marched to the spring. Marching behind him in procession were hundreds of men, women, and children. At the spring, the priest filled the pitcher with water. When he and his followers returned to the Temple, they were greeted by three blasts on ram horns and the wild cheers of the crowd waiting for them.

The priest musicians, who were lined up on the fifteen steps between the Court of the Israelites and the Women's Court, began to play as the high priest went up the ramp to the altar.

On top of the altar were two openings, one to receive a sacrifice of wine, the other to receive water. The high priest held the mouth of the pitcher over the water hole. The people did their part. "Lift up your hands!" they shouted with good humor. They wanted to make sure he poured the water directly into the water hole and not elsewhere.

The shout became part of the ceremony after the death of King Alexander Jannaeus, in 76 B.C.E. Alexander was an unpopular king. He made himself even more unpopular because he appointed himself high priest. Usually, the two offices were kept separate. Alexander had contempt for the water-pouring ritual and he let everyone know it. He poured the water not into the hole, but onto the ground. The people threw their etrogs at him to let him know what they felt.

The present high priest, however, poured as he should. The people shouted and cheered, and the musicians blew their trumpets. The people were jubilant. They clapped and stamped their

LiFt up YouR hANDs!

feet. They blessed each other, saying, *May God bless you in Zion, so you may see the goodness of Jerusalem all the days of your life.*

The choir sang *hoshanahs.* These are songs or prayers. *Hoshanah* is a contraction of two Hebrew words, *hoshiah na,* which mean "Save us, please." As the priests with willows marched around the altar the choir sang the hoshanah:

> We beseech you, God, save us, please.
> We beseech you, God, make us to prosper.

The people, who were holding branches of their own, joined in the singing, and also shook their branches.

At night, everyone went to the Temple court-yard to watch the famous torch dance. In the courtyard were three giant golden *menorahs* – oil lamps. Each had four branches, with cups for oil. Four ladders rested against the sides of each menorah. They were needed. Each menorah stood on a base that was several yards high, and the oil cups could not be reached without the ladders.

Twelve young priests, chosen for their athletic ability, came hurrying into the courtyard. Each carried a jar of oil. They climbed up the ladders at great speed and poured oil into the cups. Wicks were already burning, but the added oil sent up giant flames into the air, lighting all of Jerusalem.

Then came the dancers. Young men holding torches leaped into the courtyard. As musicians played, the dancers tossed their torches into the air, caught them again, and began to dance.

Singing and dancing went on all night long. At dawn, the musician priests brought the festivities to an end. They blew three blasts on their trumpets, telling people to go home. Some were reluctant to leave. The musicians marched down the steps and across the courtyard, playing their trumpets, escorting these people out.

The same ceremony was repeated each day for six days.

On the seventh day, the priests circled the altar not once but seven times. After the last procession, they beat their willows against the altar or on the ground.

On the eighth day it was time for the pilgrims to leave Jerusalem and return home. Before de-

parting, they gathered in the Temple courtyard to watch the smoke from the altar. Eager, and fearful, they watched to see in which direction the smoke blew. Smoke blowing north was a bad sign. It meant there would be too much rain, so that crops would be ruined. If it blew south, it meant there would be too little rain, with the same result. Everyone sighed with relief if the smoke blew east. That meant a perfect rain would fall — not too much and not too little. Smoke blowing west brought dread to every heart. That meant no rain. No rain meant drought. Drought meant famine.

According to popular belief, however, the forecast could be changed. It took the prayers of a pious individual to effect the change. Honi the Circle Maker was such a one. One Sukkot, the weather had been dry for very long. People were afraid of drought. They called upon Honi to pray for rain. Honi drew a circle around himself, sat down in it, and began to pray. He told God he would not budge from the spot until it began to rain. When a rain began to fall, Honi got up.

An Eighth Day Is Added

The Jewish sages gave the eighth day a special character. Over the seven days of the holiday the Jews offered up seventy sacrifices, on behalf of the seventy nations of the world. The sages said that on the eighth day the Jews should offer up a sacrifice from the Jews alone. In time the eighth day became the day on which to pray for rain — *geshem* in Hebrew. The eighth day was known as Shemini Atzeret, Eighth Day of Assembly.

Sukkot During the Jewish Wars

Over two thousand years ago, the Jews lost their independence to one foreign conqueror after another. Alexander the Great was an enlightened ruler, but after he died, Antiochus IV inherited Judea. This tyrant tried to force the Jews to worship his gods. The Jews revolted. They fought from 168 to 165 B.C.E. In the end, they won. In 165 B.C.E., they rededicated the Temple that Antiochus had ruined. The holiday of Hanukkah, which means "rededication," was created at this event. The Jews also celebrated Sukkot, the fall harvest festival that war had prevented them from celebrating for three years. Now they made up for it, celebrating for eight days, marching around the Temple, and holding the four species in their hands.

Later, the Jews fought another Antiochus, a more benevolent one this time. Antiochus Eusebes was called "the Pious." The Jews were led in this revolt by John Hyrcanus. In the seventh month, Hyrcanus asked Antiochus for a seven-day truce, so he and his men could celebrate the holiday. Antiochus agreed.

Later still, Rome conquered Judea and destroyed the Temple in the year 70 C.E. (Jews refer to the period Christians call A.D. as the Common Era.) In the years immediately before the destruction, the Jews minted their own coins and struck the coins with symbols of the festival, the lulav and etrog. Rome not only destroyed the Temple but razed the city of Jerusalem and drove many Jews from the land. Many who remained behind continued to fight against Rome.

From 132 to 135 C.E. the Jews again struck lulavs and etrogs on their coins. The Jews fought their last major battle against Rome in 134 C.E. It was led by Bar Kochba. When the fall festival came around, Bar Kochba sent men to bring back lulavs and etrogs for the army, so they could celebrate Sukkot. Bar Kochba was slain by the Romans. To punish the Jews, Rome changed the name of Judea to Palestine and banned all Jews from Jerusalem. Rome rebuilt the city and called it Aelia Capitolina.

Jewish coin with Temple facade and lulav with etrog

New Customs Are Added

The Jews who were driven from Palestine settled in all parts of the world. They took their festivals with them. The elaborate rituals that involved the altar, sacrifice, and water-pouring disappeared. But new customs took their place.

Holy Guests — Ushpizin

The Bible tells of the time that Abraham welcomed three strangers to his tent. He did not know they were angels. Because of this, Abraham is seen as a symbol of kindness and hospitality. In the second century C.E., the Jews had a custom of inviting Abraham into their sukkah as a symbolic guest. Many centuries later, the Jews of Spain revived the custom and enlarged it. They added other biblical guests.

The Aramaic word for guests is *ushpizin*. Spanish Jews invited seven biblical guests into the sukkah each evening. Each guest was chosen for some great quality that he possessed. All seven symbolic visitors were present. But each night another one was honored.

Abraham, the guest of the first night, represents kindness.

Isaac represents a spirit of sacrifice.

Jacob represents humility.

Joseph, the guest of the fourth night, represents wisdom.

Moses represents greatness.

Aaron, the high priest, represents holiness.

King David, who sang and wrote love songs to God, represents love of God.

The ceremony of ushpizin created a new ruling. The sages who make rules said poor people must be invited to the sukkah celebration. They explained that holy visitors would refuse to remain in a sukkah if poor people were excluded. That was the official reason. The sages used every occasion to remind people to think of the poor.

A Ninth Day— Simhat Torah

From Babylonia, an area that today includes Iraq, came another custom. The Hebrew word for Bible is *Torah*. The Torah is also thought of as a book of Law. The Torah may appear in book form or rolled up, as a scroll. Babylonian Jews followed this custom: they read the entire Torah scroll aloud in the synagogue over the year. They finished the reading on the evening of the eighth day, on Shemini Atzeret.

To celebrate, they removed all the Torah scrolls and marched joyously around the synagogue with them. The custom spread to Jews all over the world, and the parade around the synagogue became a favorite with children. The custom changed the nature of the eighth evening of Sukkot. The evening began to be called *Simhat Torah*, Rejoicing in the Torah. Gradually, the celebration became too great to be contained by one evening. So the sages added a ninth day to the holiday, to give the Simhat Torah celebration a space of its own.

How the Holiday
Is Celebrated Today

At Home

Customs vary somewhat from land to land. Even
the number of days varies. In Israel, and among
Reform Jews, the Sukkot festival is celebrated for
eight days. Orthodox and Conservative Jews celebrate for the full nine days. All home ceremonies
take place in the sukkah. This allows Jews to
imitate the way their ancestors lived and feel a
closeness to those times.

The Sukkah. One basic rule governs the building
of a sukkah: It must be a temporary structure, one
that is easy to put up and take down. Beyond that,
a sukkah may be any size, so long as it is tall
enough for grown-ups to enter. Sukkah walls may
be made of any material — boards, aluminum,
even bedsheets or carpets.

The roof has its own set of rules. It must be put on last, after the walls are standing. The Hebrew word for this particular roof is *sehach*, which means overhanging boughs or plant covering. The roof must be made of vines, branches, and plants of the earth. These are placed over a few boards or strands of fibre which act as a frame. The plants must be scattered in such a way that the people in the sukkah have shade in the daytime and a glimpse of the stars at night.

All Kinds of Sukkot. A sukkah is put up next to the house, on the roof, beside a garage, or wherever there is room. Building a sukkah is a family affair, and everyone pitches in to do his or her part. Sometimes several families decide to share a sukkah, so they build one together.

Some people go to great lengths to make a sukkah beautiful. Most are simple. A famous sukkah

is on display at the Israel Museum in Jerusalem. It was made in 1823, in Germany. The sukkah could be transported because it consists of dozens and dozens of individual panels. When the panels are raised up and placed side by side, they become a sukkah. From the outside, the sukkah looks like a charming one-room wooden house. On the inside, it is like a folk museum in itself. An artist has painted over the walls, covering them with scenes from Bible stories.

Hasidim, members of an Orthodox Jewish sect, have added a modern touch to the holiday. They have introduced the use of a "sukkah-mobile." They mount a sukkah on a truck and drive the sukkah-mobile throughout the city, stopping at schools, hospitals, and other institutions whose Jewish members may be unable to visit a sukkah. If the person can't get to the sukkah, the Hasidim bring the sukkah to the person.

Jewish soldiers in the United States Army, when they cannot get home, build a sukkah. The Office of Chief of Chaplains provides them with a manual telling them how to go about it.

People who are too busy or are "all thumbs" can order a ready-made sukkah kit from stores that sell Jewish religious articles.

Furnishings. The inside of a sukkah also varies from place to place and home to home. The furnishings reflect the way of life of the individual family.

The *Ashkinazim* are Jews whose families come

from central and eastern Europe. They will have a table and chairs in the sukkah, as they do at home. The table is covered with a cloth and set with candlesticks and candles, a lulav and etrog, wine, bread, and honey.

The *Sefardim* are Jews whose families come from Spain, Portugal, North Africa, and the Middle East. They will furnish a sukkah quite differently. Some may have a table and chairs. They may also have an extra chair, a symbolic seat for the ush-pizin. Often this will be what is called an Elijah chair, a special chair that is used at the circumcision ceremony. Since the chair is intended for the heavenly guests, holy books are put on it so that no one sits in it by mistake. Many Sefardim will have a rug on the floor in place of a table and cushions around it as chairs.

Decorations. Every sukkah is covered with decorations. They hang from the roof and adorn the wall. Children provide most of the art. Decorations range from paper cutouts to maps, flags, banners, and decorated eggs. Seasonal vegetables such as corn, peppers, carrots, gourds, and other colorful edibles are strung together to make roof hangings. Vegetable sculpture is popular. Pumpkins are given faces, with cucumbers for noses and radishes for eyes. Paper birds add to the fun, as do handwritten signs with such messages as *Bless everyone in this sukkah*; *Rejoice in your festival*; *Blessed are those who enter here*; or *Welcome Abraham* (or any of the other guests or even all of them).

Dwelling in the Sukkah. The law, as Ezra read it to the people over 2,000 years ago, said people were

to dwell in booths for seven days. That meant they were to eat, sleep, and live there, just as if they were at home. Jews living in the warm lands of the East found it easy enough to obey the law. The weather was pleasant and dry in the seventh month.

However, Jews living in other lands and in other climates found it less easy to obey the law. The sages recognized the problem and decided

Early 20th-century sukkah on New York's Lower East Side

that the ruling had to be studied and revised.

Maimonides, the great Jewish physician-philosopher of the Middle Ages, offered a new rule. He said Jews should try to eat in the sukkah whenever they could. If they couldn't actually eat there, he said that eating as little as "an olive's bulk" of bread in the sukkah fulfilled the duty. The ruling made it possible for most Jews to obey the law.

Some pious Jews insist upon obeying the more ancient law. They eat, sleep, and study in the sukkah all seven days of the holiday. Most people only eat in the sukkah and entertain friends there. Those who have no sukkah of their own will visit a sukkah long enough to say the blessings there and eat an olive's bulk of bread.

Blessings. Someone says the blessings and those gathered answer, *Amen.* All blessings begin with the same introductory words:

Ba-ruch a-tah a-do-nai El-o-hay-nu Mel-ech ha-o-lam,
Praised be God, King of the universe,

All or some of these blessings may be said:

Said upon blessing the wine

(Introductory Hebrew)
bo-ray pri ha-ga-fen.

(Introductory English)
who creates the fruit of the vine.

Said upon gathering in the sukkah

(Introductory Hebrew)
a-sher kid-sha-nu b'mitz-vo-tav v'tzi-va-nu
lay-shev ba-sukkah.

(Introductory English)
who blessed us with good teachings and commanded us
to dwell in the sukkah.

Said as bread is cut

(Introductory Hebrew)
ha-mo-tzi le-chem min ha-aretz.

(Introductory English)
who causes wheat to grow.

Said while holding the lulav and etrog

(Introductory Hebrew)
a-sher kid-sha-nu b'mitz-vo-tav v'tzi-va-nu
ahl n'ti-lat lulav.

(Introductory English)
who blessed us with good teachings, and commanded
us to take up the lulav.

Spoken to God

(Introductory Hebrew)
sheh-heh-che-ya-nu v'ki-ye-ma-nu v'hi-gi-ya-nu
la-z'man ha-zeh.

(Introductory English)
who kept us alive and allowed us to reach this season.

Said upon lighting the candles

(Introductory Hebrew)
a-sher kid-sha-nu b'mitz-vo-tav v'tzi-va-nu
le-had-lik nair shel yom-tov.

(Introductory English)
who blessed us with good teachings and
commanded us to light holiday candles.

Welcoming the Holy Guests. The ceremony welcoming the ushpizin, the biblical visitors, is performed by a member of the family. The ceremony takes place only when the family expects to eat in the sukkah and spend the evening there. No one would welcome such exalted biblical guests, then go inside to eat and leave the company "sitting" in the sukkah alone!

Today many people will include the ancient Jewish mothers in the ceremony. They welcome not only Abraham, Isaac, Jacob, Joseph, Moses, Aaron, and David. They invite also Sarah, Rebecca, Rachel, Leah, Miriam, Hannah, and Deborah into the sukkah. Some people like to make up their own speech of welcome. They may relate it to some distressing, or happy, event. Most everyone will use some version of this welcome speech.

Welcome to our meal, exalted spiritual guests (all are named). Enter (guest of the evening), holy guest from on high, enter and take your place under the protection of God. Let the beauty of God dwell among us.

Some people say, simply,

We hope and pray the world will come to live by your ways.

Although the holy guests do not eat, the Sefardim set food aside for them anyhow. They then place the food in a basket and send it to a poor family with a note saying: *This is the portion of the ushpizin.*

At the Synagogue

Jews who do not have a sukkah of their own will celebrate in the communal sukkah of a Jewish center or synagogue.

No two synagogues are exactly alike, but all will have Torah scrolls; a holy ark, the cabinet in which the scrolls are kept; and a pulpit, the platform or table from which the Torah is read.

Each morning people arrive at the synagogue with the four species. The etrog is in an etrog holder, a plain or fancy box. The three branches — willow, palm, and myrtle — are bound together with a palm leaf or carried in a woven palm holder. The trio of branches, like the palm alone, is called *lulav.*

Many sayings surround the four species. One is based on Torah study, an activity highly prized

Etrog holders from 18th-century Germany, Poland, and Holland

by Jewish scholars. The belief compares each species to a particular type of Jew. It goes like this:

Etrog (a citrus fruit) is as fragrant as the tree on which it grows. Therefore, the etrog stands for the Jew who knows the Torah and also performs good deeds.

Lulav (date palm) is sweet-tasting but without fragrance. Therefore it is like the Jew who knows the Torah but does not perform good deeds.

Hadas (myrtle) has a pleasant aroma but is not edible. Therefore it is like the Jew who does not know the Torah but does good deeds anyhow.

Aravot (willows) are neither fragrant nor fruit-bearing. They are like the Jew who neither knows the Torah nor does good deeds.

Another belief builds on this one. It says that in being bound together, the branches become a unit, and in unity there is strength.

Still another belief:

The palm resembles a spine. It says, *Stand straight and be brave.*

The myrtle leaf resembles an eye. It says, *Notice the beauty of the world.*

The willow leaf resembles a lip. It says, *Speak kindly of those around you, and praise God.*

The etrog resembles the shape of a heart. It says, *Open your heart to love and gladness.*

In the synagogue, after morning prayers, people take the lulav in their right hand and the etrog in the left. The reader, on the pulpit, praises God, saying, "Give thanks to God, for God is good and God's kindness endures forever." In reply, the people draw their right and left hands together and point with the lulav and etrog in all directions, east, west, north, and south, then up, toward the heavens, and down, at the earth. This custom is a way of saying that God reigns everywhere.

Each day people chant another hoshanah. Some hoshanahs are: God who saves, beside you there is no savior. You are powerful and able to save. God delivers and saves. Those who cry out to you – save them. Those who yearn for you – save them. Please your followers, cause an abundance of crops.

The rabbi removes a Torah scroll from the ark and stands with it on the pulpit. The *hazzan*, the cantor who leads the congregation in liturgical singing, chants the hoshanah of the day and marches around the pulpit. The people follow him. Holding lulavs and etrogs, marching in procession, they sing and make one circuit around the Torah.

After the evening prayers, people go to the synagogue sukkah. They honor the idea of dwelling in the sukkah by saying the blessings there and eating at least "an olive's bulk of bread."

The Seventh Day. On the seventh day the celebration builds to a climax. The day is called *Hoshanah Rabbah*, the Great Hoshanah, because many hoshanahs are said. In a fitting farewell to the holiday, all Torah scrolls are removed from the ark. The rabbi hands each scroll to another person. Those holding Torahs lead the congregation in seven circuits around the pulpit. The others march holding lulavs and etrogs, and chant.

Today, they have brought an additional bunch of branches to the synagogue—five willow sprigs—aravot. These are also held together with a palm leaf. When the marchers have completed seven circuits, they put aside their lulavs and etrogs and take up the willows. They beat the willows on the floor or against the back of a bench until most of the leaves have fallen off. They do it as a matter of tradition, because it is something that has always been done. It is also a symbolic act. The branches are now barren and represent a fresh start, a new beginning. Children enjoy the ceremony and bang away with great gusto. The rituals of Sukkot are now over. The lulav is no longer needed. In a spirit of fun and creativity, children tear off the leaves of the lulav and use them to make rings, bracelets, and other presents for themselves and their friends.

The seventh day is also known as the Day of Beating, or the Day of Willow Sprigs. The sages have added yet another name, Day of Help. People pray for help on that day. But the sages say the help must go in two directions. People must not only ask God for help; they must also give help to others.

Many pious Jews remain awake all night long, studying the Torah and other sacred writing.

The seventh day has given rise to many superstitions. Some people take the willow sprigs home, believing that they banish fear. One superstition says that the heavens split open on that night and that whoever sees it happen will have a dream come true. Another says that if a pregnant woman wants a boy child, she should bite off the stem of the etrog. If she wants a girl child, she merely closes her eyes and makes a wish.

The Eighth Day — Shemini Atzeret and Simhat Torah. Until now, people have thanked God for the blessings of the harvest. But there can be no harvest next year if there is no rain. According to some, the rainfall for the next year is determined on this day. People say to God, "You are the Lord our

God Who makes the wind blow and the rain fall." And they pray for a blessed rain — *geshem baruch* — not too much and not too little.

In the evening, the mood changes and a new holiday begins. It is the start of *Simhat Torah*, Rejoicing in the Torah. The Bible, or Torah, is the most precious possession of the Jews. It contains not only their ancient history but also many important teachings and poetic writings. On Simhat Torah, the rabbi once more removes all the Torah scrolls from the ark. Again he hands each scroll to another person. This night the congregation makes a minimum of seven hakafot — circuits. The people will make as many hakafot as are needed to give everyone in the synagogue a chance to march with the Torah. Those standing in the aisles and watching the parade kiss the Torah as it goes by, usually by placing a kiss on their fingertips and delivering it to the passing Torah.

The children have been looking forward to this night. It is their parade, too. Marching behind the Torah bearers, the children carry flags with the Star of David or another Jewish symbol. The flags may have an apple at the top of the pole. Sometimes the apple is hollowed out, to hold a small, lit candle. Some children may carry a miniature Torah. The smallest children participate by riding their father's shoulders.

In Orthodox synagogues, and in Israel, the joyous parade can reach great heights. It is not

שִׂישׂוּ וְשִׂמְחוּ בְּשִׂמְחַת תּוֹרָה

unusual to see men dancing with the Torah. They sing praises to God: *May the greatness of God be known forever. May the name of God be always praised.* They pray: *O God, please keep us safe. O God, please guide our ways. O God, please answer us if we call.*

The sages say it is not people dancing, but Torahs, and that people just lend their feet.

The next morning the celebration continues.

There are more hakafot around the synagogue with the Torahs. And more dancing.

What are they celebrating today? The Bible commands Jews to read the Torah. This they do in the synagogue together, each Monday, Thursday, and Saturday and on holidays. Each time they meet, they read another portion of the Torah. They finish in a year.

They celebrate because today they will read the last portion of the Torah, and finish the reading for the year. Two Torah scrolls lie open on the reading table. One is open to the beginning, the other to the end. After the hakafot, the people finish the reading. They have danced to show God how much they enjoy obeying the command to read the Torah. To emphasize the point, when they finish the reading in one scroll, they immediately begin reading the opening portion from the other, starting a new cycle of reading for the year.

The joyous atmosphere in the synagogue is almost like that of a wedding. In fact, words from the wedding ceremony are used in the reading. The man who reads the last part of the Torah is called *Hatan ha-Torah*, which means Bridegroom of the Torah. The man who reads the opening words is called *Hatan Beresheet*, Bridegroom of the Beginning. In liberal synagogues, women participate in the ceremony. The woman who reads the last part is called *Kallat ha-Torah*, Bride of the Torah. One who reads the opening words is called *Kallat Beresheet*, Bride of the Beginning.

Afterward, there is a special ceremony known as All the Lads, *Kol ha-Nearim*. A leader of the community stands on the pulpit. A prayer shawl is over his shoulders. He calls out, "All lads, come up." And all boys under the age of thirteen run to join him on the pulpit. He then opens his prayer shawl and holds it over himself and the boys, as if it were a protective tent. He then blesses them with the words Jacob used to bless his own grandchildren. The boys repeat the words after him. Then all present sing out, "Amen."

All children who are in the synagogue receive a special treat, usually paper bags filled with nuts, candies, and raisins. If the women are sitting upstairs, in the balcony, the bags will often be tossed from there.

This ceremony has led to one that includes girls as well in liberal synagogues. All children who are newly enrolled in religious school are called up to the pulpit and blessed. This merry occasion celebrates the start of their religious education.

After the evening prayers, the nine-day holiday of Sukkot is over.

Sukkot Around the World

The Middle East

The Jewish people have been separated from Palestine for almost 2,000 years. In 1948, part of Palestine became Israel, and a new Jewish state was born. The Jews had a haven and homeland again.

Many Arab lands expelled their Jewish citizens. These Jews, and others who no longer felt welcome in Arab lands, went to Israel to live. They came from Iran, Iraq, Syria, Morocco, and other Arab lands, and brought their customs with them.

The walls of their sukkot are often made of carpets or sheets. A rug on the floor will be their table. On it will be their favorite foods. They will sit or lean on cushions.

After Israel became a state, some 46,000 Yemenite Jews, in a dramatic move known as Operation

Magic Carpet, were airlifted out of Yemen in 1949–50. They were brought to Israel to live. The customs they followed in Yemen they still follow in Israel. Yemenites will often build a house leaving one room roofless. The room serves various purposes. Over the years it may be used for storage or as a guest room. At Sukkot it is covered with vines and branches and becomes a sukkah. Inside, the Yemenites sit on the floor, on mats, like the other people of Eastern lands. An entire family will often sleep together on the floor, throughout the holiday. It is a custom among them, when a little boy is brought to the synagogue for the first time on Simhat Torah, that the whole congregation blesses him.

The ancient Samaritans in Israel are small in number, only a few hundred families. They have not allowed time to change their customs. They obey the law as it is stated in the Bible. The Bible tells them to dwell in booths, and they do so. They take precautions against the weather. They build a sukkah inside the synagogue. This allows their sukkah to stand even in the face of high winds, should they occur, or heavy rains.

All Jews in Israel, no matter what part of the world they come from originally, look forward to celebrating the holiday. The weather is usually fine, warm and pleasant. And whether they sit on cushions or chairs, they enjoy spending the evening in the sukkah, amid relatives and friends.

Each group of Jews has its own synagogue, an

outgrowth of the one they attended in their former land. They go to the synagogue for the ceremonies. In Jerusalem, Jews of all backgrounds search out a rooftop or window with a view of Mount Moriah and the Mount of Olives. That is the site of the ancient Temple. Facing the hills, they pray for the well-being of their loved ones, themselves, all nations, and humankind as a whole.

Nothing remains of the ancient Temple. The only relic of those times is a section of the wall that used to surround the Temple complex. The Western Wall, as it is known, has become a holy shrine. Day and night people go there to pray. At Sukkot, they make hakafot in the open space before the wall.

Recent years have seen a unique development. Christians, led by Christian ministers, also celebrate the Feast of the Tabernacles in Jerusalem. They do so because Jesus celebrated the holiday in this place. And they have chosen this holiday because for thousands of years Jews have prayed for the welfare of Gentiles at this festival.

Russia

The government of Russia is opposed to all forms of religious expression. Jews have found it dangerous, difficult, or impossible to observe their holidays in secret. The year 1967 brought about a change. The change was not in Russian policy but in the attitude of the Jews there. That year,

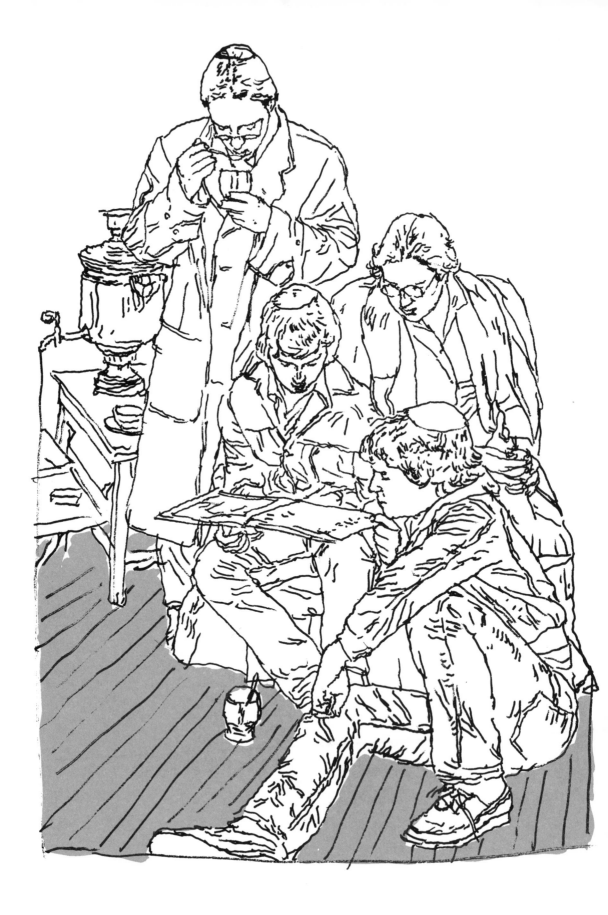

the state of Israel was attacked by Arab nations and won what is known as the Six-Day War. The ancient Jewish capital of Jerusalem, which had been divided, was united again. That gave Russian Jews a feeling of pride. They were also inspired by Golda Meir, who was Israel's ambassador to Russia and later became the prime minister of Israel.

With their newfound strength and pride, young Russian Jews began to gather at synagogues on the night of Simhat Torah. Inside the synagogue, the Torah service takes place. But outside, thousands of young Russian Jews assemble to sing Jewish and Israeli songs and to dance. It is an expression of solidarity with the state of Israel and also a form of protest. By gathering they show the Russian authorities that they openly celebrate the holiday. So far, the authorities have not interfered.

The young Jews of Moscow and Leningrad have begun another activity. Based on the Torah-reading system, they study Hebrew intensively for a year. The course ends on the night of Simhat Torah. A new course begins again the next day. As they celebrate outside the synagogue, they circulate a sign-up sheet, asking those who wish to begin the language course that starts the following day to sign up.

Russian Jews studying the Torah

Always the events of Jewish history have fashioned holiday customs. Perhaps a new custom is being born in the major cities of Russia.

Africa

The Jews of North Africa convert the balconies of their homes into sukkot by making a roof of flowers, vines, and plants. A legend exists among them. They say one can hear King David, the last of the ushpizin, playing his harp and singing on the seventh night.

The women have a custom all their own. Since men conduct the evening service in the sukkah, the women claim the sukkah for the daytime. Rachel, the wife of Jacob, is a great mother figure for the Jews. And the women of North Africa "invite" their own guest, Rachel, into the sukkah in the daytime.

Falashas are black Jews who have been living in Ethiopia from biblical times. The word *falasha* in Ethiopic means "exile" or "stranger." Some scholars believe the Falashas are one of the lost tribes of Israel, the tribe of Dan. Others say they are descendants of the son of the Queen of Sheba and King Solomon. The Falashas are very poor. They live in primitive conditions, in isolated regions. Although they are dedicated to the law of the Bible, they do not build a sukkah for the Feast of Tabernacles. Looking upon the huts in which they live the year round as symbols of the wandering of the Israelites, they spread leaves over the floor and have a special meal in honor of the Exodus of the Jews from Egypt. They also spread leaves on the floor of their synagogue, and on the last day of the holiday the religious leader carries the Torah and the people dance.

Europe

The Jews have held fast to their beliefs and traditions over the ages. Too often they have been persecuted for it. Because Jews could be found in large numbers in synagogues during holidays, a holiday was chosen as a time for attack. Jewish history is full of such episodes. Simhat Torah was chosen by a gang of Polish students in Cracow in 1648. As the Jews in the synagogue were finishing the third circuit with their Torahs, the students stormed the synagogue and massacred hundreds of Jews. A custom arose in that synagogue. Thereafter, they made only three and a half circuits on Simhat Torah. They then returned the Torahs to the ark and sat on the floor to mourn for the massacred Jews.

There were also proud moments for the Jews of Europe, as when Benjamin Disraeli was prime minister of England, in the late 1880s. Before Disraeli became prime minister, he was a writer. One day, seeing some poor Jews at the market buying willows for Sukkot, he was moved to write:

A man builds a shelter, decks it with the finest flowers and fruits, the myrtle and citron [etrog] never forgotten, and hangs it on his roof with lamps. After the service of his synagogue, he eats with his wife and children in the open air as if he were in the pleasant villages of Galilee, beneath its sweet and starry sky.

There is something profoundly interesting in this devoted observance of oriental customs in the heart of English cities, in these descendants of the Bedouins who conquered Canaan more than 3,000 years ago, still celebrating that success which secured for their forefathers the first grapes and wine.

Until World War II (1939–45), many Jews lived in small villages in eastern Europe. In Yiddish, a small village is called a *shtetl*. Shtetl Jews were very poor. Most could not afford to buy an etrog. The fruit was expensive. It was not grown locally and had to be imported, usually from the Greek island of Corfu, or from Palestine itself. At Sukkot, a few families chipped in together and bought an etrog. A messenger went from house to house with the etrog, giving each "owner" a chance to say the blessing over the fruit.

Sukkot During the Holocaust

In the long-ago days when worship took place at the Temple in Jerusalem, an entire animal was burned on the altar as a sacrifice. This was called a holocaust sacrifice. *Holocaust* means destruction by fire. In our own time, *holocaust* has come to mean a destruction of people, such as the one that took place in Europe during World War II.

The war was started by Adolf Hitler of Germany, who dreamed of conquering the world. In addition, he had one more aim — to rid the world of Jews. In each country that he conquered, his forces rounded up and arrested all! Jews.

The lucky ones, who were few in number, were sent to labor camps. There, for as long as their strength lasted, they served as slave labor in factories making equipment for Germany's war needs. Most Jews were sent to concentration camps. They were gassed to death in specially designed chambers, and their bodies were incinerated in ovens. This was the Holocaust. Hitler's armies murdered six million Jews during the war, a million of them children.

Against such a background of bestiality it is not possible to celebrate a holiday like Sukkot, which calls for joyous parades. The times were abnormal. The war was bad for all people conquered by Hitler. But the Jews were singled out for death. They knew only fear, panic, separation. It was a time when Poles, by order of the Nazis, harnessed wagons to Jews instead of to horses because it cost eighty zlotys a day to support a horse and only twenty to support a human being. So wrote Emmanuel Ringelblum in his diary before he was killed.

A child in the Terezin concentration camp, in Czechoslovakia, whose name is unknown, wrote a poem called "Homesick." One stanza says:

> Ah home, home
> Why did they tear me away?
> Here the weak die easy as a feather
> And when they die, they die forever.

Nevertheless, tradition dies hard. And when the seventh month of Tishri came around, Jews made what efforts they could to link themselves to their traditions.

In 1939 the Nazi terror was making its way across Europe. On the eve of Sukkot, the Nazis had not yet arrived in Warsaw. But they were on the way and due to arrive at any moment. Although Jews lived in dread of the Nazi arrival, they took time out of their panic to respond to a rumor. They had heard that the rabbi, Reb Meshulam, had received an etrog from Palestine. They hurried to his house. The rabbi passed the etrog around. Each one took it, said the blessing, and passed it on to the next person. The account comes from the diary of Moshe Prager, published as the book *In Sparks of Glory*.

The Warsaw Diary of Chaim A. Kaplan contains a more grim account for the seventh day of Sukkot, a few days later. By then, October 5, the Nazis had arrived. As usual, they went to look for Jews. They seized 150 during morning services at the Mlawa Street synagogue, herded them into a truck, and shipped them off to a labor camp.

"Our holiday is no longer celebrated," Kaplan wrote. "Fear has displaced gladness and the windows of the synagogue are dark."

Some accounts are more pleasant, if pathetic. The Jews at the Hassag labor camp in southern Poland, according to M. Yechezkieli, managed a secret celebration. When the guards weren't looking, the Jews put branches into an open space between two buildings, making a sukkah roof, then sat under it to eat their ration of food for the day.

Foods of Sukkot

"You shall rejoice in your festival," the Bible says. It is a command people are glad to obey. The cooks in the family take out pots and baking tins and get busy cooking. No one dish is typical to Sukkot. But certain foods are associated with holidays and celebrations, and they are certain to appear on the Sukkot table.

Hallah. Hallah is the traditional Jewish bread. It is soft and white on the inside, with a well-done crust. On Sukkot the hallah may be adorned with one of several symbols made of the same dough. One example is a ladder — to help prayers rise to heaven. The ladder may also remind people of the ladders used in the days of the ancient torch dance. Another symbol is a key — to open the gates of heaven with. A baked hand is a symbol that shows an acceptance of God's laws. A bird is a

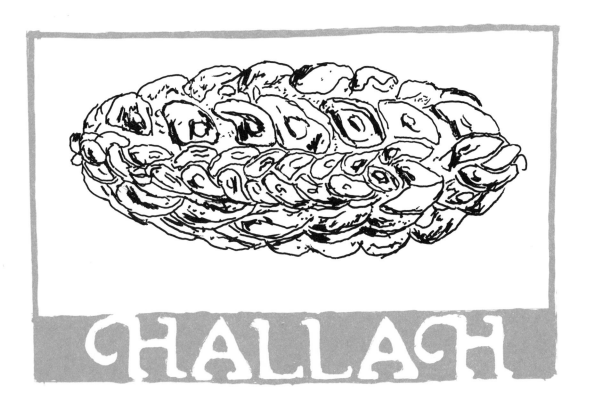

CHALLAH

symbol of protection. The idea comes from the
prophet Isaiah. Speaking to the people of God's
protection he said, "As fluttering birds, so will
God shield Jerusalem." Birds sometimes fly over
Jerusalem in such large numbers as to create the
impression that a canopy covers the city. He may
have chosen the image of a shield from that sight.

Honey. This present from the bees shows up at
every holiday and is bound to be seen at Sukkot.
Canaan, Judea, Palestine, Israel are all different
historic names for the same land. The land also
has poetic names, the Promised Land, the Holy

Land, Land of Milk and Honey. Milk and honey signify a land of plenty.

Honey cake. This appears at all festive occasions. A ladder, key, or other symbol might also be featured on the cake.

Kreplach. Kreplach are dumplings, small triangles of dough stuffed with chopped meat. They are usually served in soup. Some people say this dish is a true Sukkot dish. The reason? As willows are beaten on this holiday, so must the flour be beaten to make dough.

Teiglach. Teiglach is a sticky sweet pastry made up of small balls of dough covered with honey and nuts. This treat is favored by Ashkenazim.

Baklava. A sweet pastry of honey, nuts, and flaky dough, called baklava, is served by Sefardim on special occasions.

Etrog jam. Jam made from etrogs is eaten on Simhat Torah, if the etrog has been made into jam by then. If not, it will be eaten on the following Sabbath.

Songs

Many songs are sung throughout this long festival. Two Hebrew songs capture the spirit of the holiday. One speaks of the love of the land, the other of the joy of togetherness.

Adama

A-da-MA, a-da-MA,
bash-fay-LAH u-BA-ra-MAH
ba-ma-TAR u-ba-KHAMA
at i-MAY-nu, a-da-MA,
aim a-DAM
ad-MAT kol KHAI.

Mother Earth

Mother earth, mother earth,
all your valleys and hills,
in times of rain or shine,
you are our mother, earth,
and mother
of all that lives.

Hinay mah tov

Hi-NAY ma TOV
u-ma NA-YIM
she-VET a-KHIM gam
YA-KHAD

How Good It Is

How good it is
and how pleasant
to be with each other,
oh yes.

An English song for Simhat Torah expresses
the meaning of the holiday:

Earth with All Thy Thousand Voices
Earth with all thy thousand voices,
praise in songs to God our king.
To God who gave us our Torah,
let us ever praises bring.
Hold aloft that sacred Torah,
read within it all you can.
Learn its lessons, learn to live them,
teach its laws to every man.

Some Jewish Terms and Their Meanings

Altar The fireplace in the courtyard of the Tabernacle on which animals were sacrificed in ancient times.

Ark The cabinet in a synagogue in which Torah scrolls are kept.

Beating willows In ancient times, people beat willow branches against the ground to call forth rain. They also used the willows to beat themselves, and each other, in a fertility ceremony.

Circuits (Hakafot) People marching in procession around a central place — the altar in ancient times, the pulpit today. Ancient people (and some modern people, too) believed a circle possessed magic, that it was a protected place that evil spirits were afraid to enter. A circle thus came to stand for a place of safety. The hakafot around the altar are a form of circle.

Covenant The treaty between God and the Jewish people. The first treaty was made with Abraham and Sarah, and renewed with Moses and the Jews of his time. God promised the Jews to make a nation of them, and to give them Canaan (Israel today) as a homeland. In return, the Jews promised to worship only God and to keep the laws that Moses brought down from Mount Sinai. The Ten Commandments are also known as the Covenant.

Elijah's chair An ornamental chair used in the circumcision ceremony. Elijah was a Hebrew prophet in the ninth century B.C.E. He fought to rid the land of idol worship. According to popular belief, he did not die but rather ascended to heaven in a fiery chariot. Many Jews think Elijah will return to earth prior to the arrival of the Messiah. He is therefore seen as a messenger of good tidings.

Four species The four types of plant life used in the Sukkot festival ceremony: palm, willow, myrtle, and etrog.

Menorah A many-branched lampstand with cups of oil or candles. A seven-branch menorah is the symbol of the state of Israel.

Priests In the days of the Temple, Jewish religious services were conducted by priests. After the destruction of the Temple, priests were replaced by rabbis.

Rabbi A Hebrew word that means "my teacher." The rabbi is a religious leader.

Sacrifice The animal, vegetable, or wine that was offered up to God on the altar. Sacrifice is an ancient form of prayer.

Seven This number has great significance in Jewish life. God made the world in six days and rested on the seventh. The seventh day is the Jewish Sabbath. Joshua circled the walls of Jericho seven times. Jewish mystics say there are seven heavens between earth and the heavenly realm of God.

On the seventh day of Sukkot, Jews make seven circuits around the synagogue. Jewish festivals are often seven days long.

Shade Shade and water are two themes of Sukkot. Both are blessings, and God is believed to be the bestower of all blessings. The sukkah, which offers shade, is seen as a form of protection.

Synagogue A Greek word meaning "house of assembly." At the time synagogues came into being, Greek was the main language of the known world. A synagogue is a Jewish house of worship, study, and assembly.

Tabernacle A tent used as a portable shrine by the Israelites during their desert wandering.

Temple The house of worship that King Solomon built and dedicated to God in 955 B.C.E. in Jerusalem to replace the portable Tabernacle. The Temple was destroyed by the Romans in 70 C.E.

Sukkot Glossary

There is a sound in the Hebrew language that does not exist in English. It is sometimes spelled in English with an *h* and sometimes with *ch*, but neither comes close. The sound in Hebrew is similar to the sound made when you clear your throat. But it is softer and more refined. In the pronunciation guide below the sound is spelled *kh*.

Aravot (ah-rah-VOTE) Willow branches

Arba minim (ar-BAH me-NEEM) Four species

Ashkenazim (ash-ken-ah-ZIM) Jews from central and eastern Europe

Etrog (et-RUG) One of the four species, a citrus fruit

Geshem baruch (GEH-shem ba-RUKH) Blessed rain

Hadas (ha-DAHS) Myrtle branch, one of the four species

*Hag Aliyat ha-regel (khag ah-li-*YAT ha-REH-gel) Walking, or Pilgrim, Festival

Hag ha-Asif (khag ha-a-SEEF) Festival of Ingathering

Hag ha-Elohim (khag ha-el-o-HEEM) Festival of the Lord

Hag ha-Sukkot (khag ha-sue-KOTE) Festival of Booths

Hakafot (ha-ka-FOTE) Circuits, or people marching in circles

Hallah (kha-LA) A braided white bread

Hasidim (kha-si-DEEM) An Orthodox Jewish sect

Hatan ha-Torah (kha-TAN ha-tow-RAH) Bridegroom of the Torah, the name given to those who read the last portion of the Torah

Hatan Beresheet (kha-TAN b'ray-SHEET) Bridegroom of the Beginning, the name given to those who read the first portion

Hazzan (kha-ZAHN) Singer of liturgical songs

Hoshanah (ho-SHA-nah) A type of prayer. The term is a contraction of two words, *hoshiah na*, meaning, "save us, please."

Hoshanah Rabbah (ho-SHA-nah rah-BAH) Great Hoshanah — the seventh day of Sukkot, because of the many hoshanahs sung that day

Kallat Beresheet (kah-LAT b'ray-SHEET) Bride of the Beginning

Kallat ha-Torah (kah-LAT ha-tow-RAH) Bride of the Torah

Kol ha-Nearim (kol ha-ne-ah-REEM) All the Lads, a ceremony performed on Simhat Torah

Kreplach (KREP-lakh) A meat-filled dumpling

Lulav (lu-LUV) One of the four species, a palm branch. Also the name for the set of three species of palm, myrtle, and willow.

Sehach (s'KHAKH) The plants used for the roof of the sukkah

Sefardim (s'far-DEEM) Jews from Spain, Portugal, North Africa, and the Middle East

Shemini Atzeret (sheh-mi-NEE ah-TSERET) Eighth Day of Assembly, the eighth day of Sukkot

Shofar (show-FAHR) Ram's horn, an ancient trumpet

Simhat Bet ha-shoevah (sim-KHAT bait ha-SHOW-eh-VAH)
Rejoicing over the Water Drawing, an elaborate
Temple festival which began each morning with
the water-drawing ritual and ended at night with
the torch dance

Simhat Torah (sim-KHAT tow-RAH) Rejoicing in the
Torah, the ninth day of Sukkot. The yearly reading of the Torah is finished and begun anew on
this day.

Sukkah (sue-KAH) The temporary booth used on the
holiday Sukkot

Sukkot (sue-KOTE) The name of the holiday, and the
plural of *sukkah*. It is also the place where the
fleeing Israelite slaves stopped for the first time
as a free people.

Teiglach (TAYG-lakh) A pastry of honey and nuts

Torah (tow-RAH) The sacred scroll in the synagogue;
Jewish law; the Bible

Ushpizin (oosh-pi-ZEEN) The biblical guests who are
invited to the sukkah: Abraham, Isaac, Jacob,
Joseph, Moses, Aaron, King David

Zeman Simhatenu (z'MAHN sim-kha-TAY-nu) Festival
of Rejoicing

Other Books About Sukkot and Simhat Torah

Adler, David A. *The House on the Roof.* New York: Bonim Books, 1976. Illustrated by Marilyn Hirsh. A storybook for young children about an old man who builds a sukkah on the roof—against the landlord's wishes.

Cedarbaum, Sophia N. *Sukos and Simchas Torah.* New York: Union of American Hebrew Congregations, 1961. A basic book with board covers for very young children. Debbie and Danny experience the holiday in the synagogue, in the sukkah, and during the Simhat Torah parade.

Drucker, Malka. *Sukkot.* New York: Holiday House, 1982. For ages 8 to 12, a companion to the author's other Jewish holiday books.

Goodman, Philip. *The Sukkot and Simkhat Torah Anthology.* Philadelphia: Jewish Publication Society, 1973. A comprehensive, thorough, all-inclusive anthology—history, stories, customs, writings, crafts.

Schauss, Hayyim. *The Jewish Festivals.* New York: Schocken Books, 1962. A full and lively history of all Jewish festivals. Paperback.

Index